Jewelry Making

Crush it in the Jewelry Making Business

Make Huge Profits by
Designing Exquisite
Beautiful Jewelry
Right In Your Own Home

Table of Contents

Introduction

Earning money is a basic necessity in life and most of us are looking for a way to earn money doing something that we love. The sad truth is that most people live their whole lives working a dead end job for people that they don't like and doing work that they hate just to get that paycheck at the end of the month. Why put yourself through all that stress when there are alternatives?

What is your passion in life and, do you think it has a business potential? Ask any millionaire the key to becoming wealthy and happy and they will tell you that, hands down, you need to do what you love and add value to people's lives, and wealth and abundance are bound to follow.

There are many activities which people find enjoyable but that can also can be very profitable. Drawing, designing, teaching, and writing: all if these are passions that can be turned into a full time job. And it just so happens that all of these jobs can also be taken up from your home office. It's great being able to take care of your family and to relax whenever things get too much.

Another hobby that can turn into a great source of income is jewelry making. If you have even the most basic knowledge in beading, smithing, and wire-working, then you have the potential to be a stay-at-home business owner! What you need is just the correct mindset and knowledge. It turns out that there's an ever hungry market of people who are always looking for something unique to wear and all it takes it some creativity from a jewelry maker to make it happen!

This book is for you if you want some insight into jewelry making techniques and want to know how to use these techniques to set up a profitable business. Having a successful business selling jewelry is about more than just having the best designs. In this book, how to go about promoting your new jewelry business and making it a complete success.

From the basic knowledge, benefits, and to understanding your own styles and strengths, this book has you covered. If you're ready to become your own boss, take complete control of your schedule, and take better care of your work-life balance, turn to the next page!

I'll see you on the flip-side.

Chapter 1: The Basic Knowledge You Need

As with any other business, one must be equipped with the proper knowledge before even thinking of opening for sales. One can say that getting the knowledge is easy, what with the Internet being the heart and soul of information nowadays. The problem is that there is such a wealth of information out there that it will take you ages to sift through it yourself. In business, time is money so I have laid out what you need to know now, with no flowery language - just good solid advice.

Running a jewelry business has its own unique challenges and we will work through these in this book. The basic business rules do still apply and you need to keep these in mind also, especially if you are planning to grow your business well over the long term.

Even if you are currently great at making jewelry, there is a huge difference between making the odd gift or two for friends and actually making enough for a craft show or business. Whilst your craft skills will help when it comes to creating your jewelry, you also need some general business know-how as well.

Many people start a small jewelry business because they think that it is easy. They rush in enthusiastically without doing any research upfront and then end up sitting with product that they cannot move because they didn't know how to market their products or because they did not take enough time to get to know their market.

Here are the basics of Jewelry Making Business that you should know about:

A Great Business Name

You already make great pieces, your friends go gaga over the gifts you need them - surely that is enough? Except that it really is not. In order to build a sustainable business, you will need to think about branding from day one.

Think of some of the brands that you know and love - you will buy their products without question most of the time, won't you? That is because they have taken time and trouble to build a positive brand image. The same must be done for any small business.

A great brand starts with a great business name. The name needs to be striking and easy to remember. "McPherson's Beauty Emporium", for example, sounds really good and has a sound of class to it. Makes a great name, doesn't it?

Well, actually no. First of all, it is way to long and contains too many words that are harder to spell. Think about it for a second - your clients need to be able to remember your brand name in order to be able to recommend you to their friends.

The name is not easy to spell and you may lose out if people try to find your brand online.

Also, the words "Beauty Emporium" will create a little confusions when it comes to what it is that you actually do.

The name must be striking, easy to remember and unambiguous.

Look at "Honey Jewelry" for example. That is a great name because we know straight away that they sell jewelry, the name is really simple to remember and easy to spell but, more than all of that, it is striking and unusual.

Look for a simple, elegant solution when it comes to naming your business.Keep in mind that your packaging, your business cards, and your website will carry that name. Names do matter, so make your business name count.

This does bear a little careful thought so go ahead and do a draft logo and some mock up stationary - this is easily done in most word processing programs. Canva.com has plenty of free templates that you can play around with as well. How does the name look in black and white?

The reason that is important to spend some time with this because this is nothing something that you can easily change a few months down the line. Changing your business's name is something that should not be undertaken lightly as it can destroy all the branding efforts that you have made.

Once you have decided on the name, Google it and see if there are other companies with the same name. In some instances, companies go to the trouble of patenting their names and logos and can be quite aggressive when it comes to people who have copied them. A unique name is the best way to go.

Choosing a name that resembles that of a large company is a pretty weak strategy anyway - people will realize that you are trying to ride the coattails of the larger company and wander what else you are faking.

Basic Tools and Your Workplace

It is best to set aside a workspace in your home where projects can be left undisturbed when not being worked on. Have a door that locks so that your family understands that you are unavailable during working hours. This is the main disadvantage of working from home - it is easy for the lines to blur and you may find that your family and friends become a big distraction. Fortunately, this can be handled by being firm and, politely, insisting that they respect that you are at your home office, not at leisure.

You do not need a huge workspace but do make sure that the area is very well lit and that you have a comfortable chair that allows you to maintain good posture when you are working.

You also want a room that is easily ventilated - you may need to use strong glues from time to time.

The space must be kept clean and organized. Find spaces to put all your tools in and make sure that you always put your things away in the same place. By getting into the habit of doing this, you will always know where things are if you need to find them in a hurry. This becomes more important when you are working under a tough deadline.

There are a lot of fun toys that you can buy but refrain from buying too much equipment, at least at first. You can always buy more tools at a later stage as needed. You also need to consider what you will be making as this will have a great influence on what you need to buy.

To start off with, make use of simple beading supplies - you do not need to jump into making sterling silver jewelry or buying any expensive machinery when starting out.

Start with the following basic tools:

Pliers: You will need at least two pairs of pliers - one pair should be needle-nose and the other should be plain. Pliers are incredibly useful and can be used to create findings, coil and wrap wire, etc. They can also be very helpful when it comes to getting a hold on little fiddly bits for jewelry making. I also find that they are a great substitute for a crimping tool. I, too this day have never bothered to buy a crimping tool.

Workbench: You can use an old desk as well. Do consider the height of the desk and whether or not you need to stoop in order to work at it. If this is the case, you should consider using some storage cubes to raise the work surface that you are working on.

Wire Cutters: If you are going to be working with jewelry wire, you will need to have wire cutters. Keep these nice and sharp and use only on your jewelry projects.

Storage Boxes: If possible, buy these in bulk to save some cash. You will need a lot of these to help organize the different findings and bead

A Magnifying Glass On a Stand: This is not strictly necessary but it can come in useful when doing intricate work.

An Adjustable Desk Lamp: Again, not absolutely necessary but also very useful when working on fine projects.

Scissors: You will need scissors in order to cut the tiger tail or nylon you will be using.

A Beading Mat: These are easy to make yourself so don't buy the expensive variety. The beauty of these mats is that the beads don't slip and slide all over them. I made mine by getting a large old frame from a thrift store. I removed the glass and the backboard. I covered the backboard with a piece of felt and glued it in place and then returned it to the frame. Test that the backboard will still fit into the frame when the felt has been applied before you actually glue the felt down. The frame will stop the beads dropping all over the place if you knock something over.

A Beading Board: These are inexpensive and I feel that it is worthwhile to get two in different sizes. These boards are a good buy as they will help you to plan your design and also hold the beads in place at the same time.

And that is pretty much all you need to get. More than that is really not necessary, until you become more experienced and know what you are doing. For absolute beginners, I recommend buying a kit and practising on this first - the kit should have detailed instructions and will enable you to learn several different techniques as well.

When starting out, I caution against buying too much in bulk, at least to start with. You might end up with a cupboard full of beads. To start off with, buy only enough to make a few items of your chosen projects. It is more expensive to buy this way but you can look at buying in bulk when you have a better idea what will and will not sell.

There Are Still Risks

Just because you're working at home, doesn't mean that there are zero dangers. Due to the measured and small movements, you and those working with you can suffer from hand pain and injuries such as Carpal Tunnel Syndrome, Tendinitis, and Repetitive Strain Injury. Stabbing yourself with sharp objects is also a risk.

Another danger that you might encounter is when the stones you have picked are bombarded with lead. This often happens when business owners want to cost-cut and resort to buying unbelievably inexpensive stones, not knowing that their low price is due to the health dangers that come with them. Dealing with reputable dealers will help here. Also keep an eye out for deals that seem too good too be true - if the stones are a whole lot cheaper than similar ones, there is a good chance that they are low grade or even dangerous.

Make sure to give your hands regular breaks and also do wrist exercises to reduce the risk of injury. If you are cutting or grinding stones, or working with heat, always be sure to wear safety glasses and gloves.

You are going to end up, at some stage or another, cutting or burning yourself. Have a small first aid kit on hand to deal with these little injuries.

Building Your Practical Skills

Even if you are skillful, you must accept that, prior to opening a Jewelry Making Business, that you have to update your skill-set. From time to time you will need to attend seminars and classes that aim to widen your creativity and skill level. You can find a number of free video tutorials on YouTube that will make it possible to learn new techniques.

Your styles may do well now, but people's wants change and you need to be ready for this. What is hot and trendy today may be completely overdone tomorrow. Take some time to search out jewelry makers magazines for updates on buyer wants and new improved techniques. Most important of all, get feedback from your clients themselves about new things that they might be interested in seeing on your shelves.

Expanding Your Portfolio

Lastly, work on building your portfolio by updating it regularly. Have a camera ready with you and take photos of your creations, ensuring that the light is as good as possible and that the goods are shown in their best light. (You can crop the photos and maybe make small adjustments to the contrast or brightness but do make sure that the photos are still an accurate representation of the product.

Keep a digital file of all your photos and make sure to display them on your website - with captions naming the design and materials used.

If you will also be selling at craft fairs, it might pay to have the photos developed and to put them in a nice album so that you can refer to them at the fairs - clients can then place orders.

Make sure that you keep your catalogs and website up to date and do change the photos on your brochures and pamphlets regularly so that regular clients can see the new stuff that you are doing as well .

Also consider posting the pictures to social media sites such as Pinterest and Facebook with a link to your site to get even more exposure.

Chapter 2: Jewelry Making At Home

As the popular passage states, pick the work you love and you'll never have to work a day in your life. For those who already love jewelry making, then having this business is perfect! For those who know nothing about it, then starting it may actually cause you to fall in love with it. It is a very creative endeavor and can be deeply satisfying as well.

Working From Home Does Have A Lot Of advantages

You basically get to set your own schedule so there is no need to ask permission of anyone if you need a day off or an extra-long lunch break. There is also no long commute to work and no need to worry about what mood the boss is in.

You get to work and be around your family - you will have time to be there for the smaller things in life that you would have missed had you been going to an office.

The work you do is your own and so you get full credit for it - there is no need to make someone else rich through working hard. The harder you work, the better you'll do and you will reap the rewards.

Setting your own hours allows you to take advantage of when you are most productive. I, for example, are not a morning person at all so I schedule my work day to start around 10:00 am. I finish working a lot later but get a whole lot more accomplished.

Fusion of Work and Hobby

What's more enticing that doing what you love and earning money for it? Jewelry making allows you to do something that you love and to express your own personality at the same time.

It is not all going to be fun - at times it will be downright tedious (like when you are making twenty bracelets all the same) - but it is still way more fun than sitting in an office all day and hardly ever seeing the sun.

There is one fact that you will need to accept though - doing something as a hobby and doing it as a business are two completely different things. In the first instance, you do what suits you, in the second, you do what suits the customer. In order to be successful, you will need to consider what your clients want and put your own desires in terms of product design, etc. second.

Also, making one necklace a day can be exhilarating. How will you feel if you need to make ten a day? Or twenty? A business developed as a result of a hobby is still a business and a lot more effort will be required on your part.

It's a Highly Healthy Business

No more stress from missed deadlines, fewer hurried meals. Since you are working from home, and you answer to no one except your clients, you can more easily adopt a healthier lifestyle. You can choose to eat more healthy meals and take some time to exercise as well.

It can also be very satisfying to see something that you have created being appreciated by someone else.

Chapter 3: The Downside of Working From Home

Whilst it is true that there are a lot of benefits to working from home, there are also some disadvantages that can crop up. Fortunately forewarned is forearmed and these issues can be dealt with with a little forward planning.

The Death of Steady Paychecks

I'm an not going to kid you - it will be tough, especially at first. Most new businesses are not profitable enough to allow the owner to draw a salary for at least the first six months to a year.

A lot of people are scared of having their own business because of this reason: It is too uncertain. But think of it more deeply, EVERYTHING nowadays is full of uncertainty. Even the steady paycheck you are receiving can fail should recession hit the company you are working for.

Think of it this way: It is true that you will not get rich in jewelry making overnight, but same can be said when you work for someone else as well. People who are their own bosses reap the harvests (more time, flexible schedule, etc) as soon as they start the business, but being with an employer ties you down your whole life!

If you'll work really hard in Jewelry Making, you may become rich in 10 years, may be even 5. It completely depends on you. But work hard in someone else's company and see where you will be in 5 year's time. If you're really talented and you work hard, you may get promoted. BUT YOU ARE COMPETING WITH A LOT OF EMPLOYEES! The final decision is still not yours to make.

It may be hard to swallow, but it's the truth. We're not telling you to quit your day job right away, but you might as well be building your own business now.

If you are not sure, start your jewelry business on a part-time basis. This will allow you to get a feel for it without needing to leave the safety of your current job. Save as much as you can so that you have a bit of a safety cushion saved up for when you make the final switch.

The Buck Stops With You

You make all the decisions so there is no one to blame if things don't work out - you will need to handle the responsibility and this can be a hard adjustment for people to make.

Making all the decisions is not always as much fun as it is made out to be.

If you employ staff, your decisions affect them and, basically, their livelihood is in your hands. It is a fair deal of responsibility.

No More Paid Leave, Sick Leave, Etc

When you work for yourself, you don't get to call in sick. Owning a business is hard work. Yes, you will be setting your own schedule but this generally means working on some aspect of the business every day of the week, especially when it comes to getting it off the ground.

You may need to work your butt of and will probably even miss having set working hours but I can assure you, the hard work pays off big time - at least you know that all the hard work is for your own benefit.

The Bills Still Need to be Paid

This is probably the scariest part of running your own business - your bankers still want the mortgage, etc. paid on time and you might be dealing with cash flow issues. This can be tough to handle when starting out and can be nerve-wracking.

Chapter 4: Traditional VS. Modern Methods - What's Effective?

It is always the first step that's the hardest on. When starting out your own jewelry business, you're probably thinking: how do I begin? I now have the name, I have even designed a logo, but what of the jewelry? The next step is to decide what techniques you will use to make your own jewelry.

Traditional jewelry making is not that hard - you need to design your piece, either from plain metal or using gemstones. You plan the design and effect it. Traditional jewelry tends to be very symmetrical with elegant lines and using matching stones. It tends to focus on making the stones used the focal point.

Sounds boring? Not really. In fact, traditional jewelry making is very challenging. Dealing with precious metals is not as easy as it sounds. For example, pure gold is too soft to make jewelry out of so it needs to be mixed with some sort of alloy.

If you are making the pieces from scratch, a lot of time needs to be spent on creating the mould for the piece and getting the details right so that it looks great when cast. Starting up in this kind of business can be expensive and you will need to undergo specialized training in order to make jewelry that lasts well and that looks good.

The cut and color of the stone used and the setting that it is placed in will all have an impact on how well it reflects light and it is your job as a jeweller to bring out that natural beauty.

More modern techniques address the issue of costs in jewelry making and allow you to save money because you substitute the more precious metals in areas where the metal is not going to be seen - the back of the pendant, for example,

Modern techniques also make extensive use of electro-plating and such techniques in order to save money by using only a coating of precious metal on the outside of the piece of jewelry.

Now, for the question, what's effective? The answer is vague, but very true: it depends on a lot of factors. What's your budget? What's your target market? What are your means of doing the jewelry?

If you can purchase pure gold and you already have fantastic designs ready, then go ahead! A lot of people invest in pure jewels because their value increases over time. However, if you want to cater to people who buy jewelry as a part of their fashion, you can cost cut on the metals (but not to the point of low quality), and concentrate more on designs.

You will also need to consider whether or not you have the skills needed to create your own jewelry bases, etc, from scratch. This can be rather a lot more work than most people realize and is something that is better left until you have gained more experience.

Modern jewelry making allows you to dabble in a bit of both - you can create your own styles and designs but use fittings and fixtures that you have purchased. My advice for those looking for a quick and easy saleable product is to stick to techniques such as beading to begin with.

Chapter 5: Most Common (In-Demand) Techniques

To help you decide on what technique to use, let's list some of the most common jewelry making techniques that most business owners began with:

Precious metal clay: Precious metal clay was really only developed in the early 90's so it is a pretty new medium. As the name suggests, if you choose this, what you'll have is clay made from powders or dusts of precious metal, most commonly gold, silver and platinum. This does allow for some very creative and unique projects.

Can you do this at home? Yes, but it might not be very convenient. Precious Metal Clay or PMC needs fire to be properly set, so you'll need a kiln. A kiln takes up quite a bit of space and the firing needs a lot of time. Running a kiln can be an expensive business and it can be a dangerous one if you have small kids in the house.Some jewelry makers compromise by making small pieces: in doing so, they will just use butane torch, similar to what cooks use in glazing food.

Silver smithing: Silver smithing is probably one of the most popular method used by jewellers at home. In this technique, you will need special hammers or pliers to bend strips and pieces of metals and connect them together. The connection can be secured by adding rivets, staples or even glue. These are known as cold-connections and are a great way to create a more modern looking effect. This method is especially effective for steam punk looks. . Alternatively, you can also use a kiln to fire the connection.

Silver smithing requires patience and knowledge, and if you're not experienced in this method, you will really have to attend seminars and classes.

Can you make wonderful pieces that will sell? Of course! Is this the easiest method for a beginner to start off on -No.

Beading: Beading is the simplest and possibly also the easiest method, that's why most start up jewelry making businesses begin with this one. In this method, all you need is to have a wonderful plan on how to set the beads out together. And don't forget to invest in high quality beads. This is also one of the most versatile methods to use. You can make two pieces using the exact same design and have them look completely different by using different beads.

This is a good way to enter into jewelry making as it can be as simple as stringing a bead onto a piece of nylon. You can easily and inexpensively access beading supplies and can appeal to higher class of client by incorporating more high quality beads. Beads come in a range of different materials - wood, acrylic, metal, bone, etc. You can even make your own out of paper. Beads also come in a range of beautiful colors and styles.

If you are starting out, beading is the simplest way and the way that will cost the least in terms of both money and skills required.

Polymer Clay: Is a method that also needs heat, but, in this case, your own standard cooking oven will do as the clay will set at much lower temperatures. Most of the clays will cook at the temperature of 325 degrees. Just a simple reminder, though. Polymer clay may damage your wood surface, so be sure to work with it on a protected surface, preferably on ceramic surfaces.

And another thing, clays need to be conditioned. You can do it by hand or using a specialized machine - this looks like a pasta maker and makes the process of softening the clay a whole lot easier. Basically to condition the clay, you have to knead it until it becomes soft and pliable.

This can be a reasonably inexpensive way to enter the market and does allow for a fair bit of creativity. It is not a bad material for beginners to work with and is relatively inexpensive.

Wire-work: Wire-work is quite an interesting field and requires a bit of research into techniques and a bit of practice to get used to working with the wire. The advantage is that you can use wire-work to create findings and fittings for beading projects. As the name implies, you work with wire.

The downside here is that you will need to consider using silver wire and this can be pricey. I would personally advise you to go to the hardware store and get a few yards of plain old galvanized wire - about a .20 gauge if possible and practice on that. If you enjoy that, you can work you way to the more expensive wires.

The upside is that you can create truly unique, one of a kind pieces.

Green jewelry: No. It's not about making pieces from organic materials. The reason that it is termed to as green is because of the fact that you will recycle materials to come up with a fine piece. For example, coins can be melted and molded, media albums and gold scraps can be used too.

The good part is that you don't need much money to start with. The hard part is that you need to be quite creative to start from the scratch. If this does interest your, go to YouTube and look for videos on up-cycling.

Chapter 6: Why Jewelry Making can be Financially Profitable

Less Issues with Work and Storage Space

While others need to pay rent for offices, you can start right at home. Just organize your room to be a conducive workplace by having a separate area for your PC, a book or computer spreadsheet to track sales, a safe place to keep your work and a decent area where you can place your finished products for picture taking.

Everything else can be accomplished online - from promoting your work through to selling it. You will need to be willing to put some time into setting up and organizing your website and/ or social media accounts. If you do not want to go to the expense of setting up your own website, you can open a store on a commerce website like eBay or Etsy or link up to one of the sites that provide you with a store template and allow you to manage your own store, with its own domain, etc. like Shopify.com.

Being really organized is going to be essential when your business takes off so make sure that you are very careful about your admin from day one. Set up a folder on your computer for your business and in this have sub-folders for orders, for great feedback, for complaints, for proof of deliveries,sales reports, etc. so that you can find any information you need quickly when you need it. You must back up this folder on a daily basis - don't skip it or you risk losing all your hard work.

You also need space to store your inventory once it has been photographed and a good stock checking system in place. You should know what it is that you have available to sell at all times.

Imagine how much money you will save in not needing an office, This helps to make your price a whole lot more competitive. Even better, you can claim a portion of the household power bill, cleaning and mortgage. as a business expense on your taxes. (It has to be a portion appropriate to the size of your space - so if your office takes up 1/12 of the house, you can claim 1/12 the expenses as well.

Sell Your Designs

Selling your designs is also an option. For example, should the customer want to have a unique piece, offer to design the jewelry for him or her. Of course, tell the customer that there is an additional cost for the unique design as you will no longer be using it for other pieces.They then take the design on to their jeweller to be made up.

Similarly, if you still do not have the capability to open your own store, you might want to consider designing for other jewelry shops.

Your Starting Capital

Unlike other businesses, starting a jewelry making can be relatively inexpensive. That means you don't have to be taken to the cleaners just for you to begin a business. You just have to plan very carefully when it comes to the following:

Great designs sell a lot: Your design more then anything else is what will attract your client to the jewelry to start off with. If you can come up with a great design, partner that with good quality beads and great workmanship, you will be able to sell your pieces.

The key here is to make sure that even though your materials are not worth hundreds of dollars, they can still be used for a long time. You want to use a better quality when it comes to your base materials and want to ensure that you do things properly. Don't skimp when it comes to quality - if the beads start peeling or the clasp breaks the second time the person wears it, you will not get repeat business and will develop a bad name.

The Power of Social Media: Most start-up businesses from home do not have enough money to set up their own websites right away. If you have the money, it's easy to pay for the monthly hosting charge, even easier to pay for the domain name, but the difficult part is setting up the website itself. If you are not knowledgeable in web design, you will need to hire someone who is capable. But even after all that, what sort of portfolio will you put in it?

For now, rely on social media. Prepare a separate album for your works and dedicate time into sharing them with your followers or friends. No need to worry about costs because it's free! You should also consider listing your goods on Etsy or eBay as these have huge client bases and you only pay if your piece sells.

Even if you are only running a social media site, do not discount the value of Facebook ads. These ads can be launched for a few dollars and you can set your target market to suit you.

Your pieces won't perish: Should your pieces not sell for some reason (perhaps the one who reserved them suddenly needed the money for something), you don't need to worry about your work going off. These are not perishable goods. They can stay in their box until the day someone buys them. That means you won't lose money as easily as you would if you were selling food items. (And no weight gain from having to eat "mistakes" either.)

Choose Your Own Hours (Full-time/Part-Time/Seasonal)

One of the best reasons why Jewelry Making Business is financially profitable is because of your independence when it comes to dedication. Perhaps you love your job and it pays you just right so you don't want to quit it, but you still want to start a business. Jewelry making is perfect as a part time business or even a seasonal venture.

Take your days off and start planning or designing. Come up with great pieces and start posting pictures of these on your social media account. You can post the price and a bit of a description as well and leave it up to people to send you a message to arrange payment.

Don't Discount Direct Marketing

There is a reason that companies such as Avon and Tupperware are so successful - think about it, they don't really go out and find their own clients, they actually have people paying to sign up with them and being agents. The agents pay for everything they order - from product to the very bags to pack goods in. You can take a lesson from this in one of two ways.

See if people that you know are willing to host jewelry parties - in exactly the same way as they would host a Tupperware party. You provide the snacks, prepare a little sales pitch, set up games to play and the hostess provides the guests. You give your hostess a thank you gift - usually the higher the sales made, the bigger the gift and everyone is happy.

Alternatively, find people that you know and trust who are looking to earn some extra money. You will need to work in a rewards system for them but it will work in much the same way as Avon does - on a commission basis - you'll give each agent a catalogue that they can then use as a sales tool. Do make sure that the copies are really good. Also let them have a sample of merchandise like a bracelet or something that they can use to show the people what the workmanship is like. In need, you can give the actual goods out in place of a catalogue but this might be a bit of a risk unless you know the person really well. As far as possible. rather let them get orders for goods and have the clients either pay the whole amount or a deposit up front.

Direct marketing in this manner can expose you to a whole new range of clients whilst cutting back on your workload in terms of finding clients to sell to.

You should, however, charge the same prices to the general public as your reps do and arrange performance bonuses to keep them motivated.

Chapter 7: Business Opportunities for Jewelry Making

Most of us think that to make it big in business we need to start out with a huge whack of capital and that we need to have the best and most expensive of everything. It is this thinking that puts so many of us off starting our own businesses. In fact, it is this thinking that ensures that we pretty much will never make it big in business.

Look at the business success stories today - Richard Branson has made billions, lost it all and then done it all again. Read his biography and you will see that he never let anything as unimportant as a lack of capital stand in his way.

Instead of delaying the business, why not start with the money that you have right now. Look creatively at making your budget stretch. Why not take a trip to your local thrift store and see what you can find there? You can often pick up old necklaces for pennies - often with the beads still in good shape. Consider alternative sources for supplies - fishing gut is usually a whole lot cheaper than beading wire and they are practically the same thing.

Innovation will pay great dividends throughout the life of your business and allow to save money and come up with great alternative solutions without looking cheap.

Keep your eyes open for opportunities and they will come your way.

Seasonal Advantages (You can never go wrong with jewelry as gifts!)

People want to give their loved ones special gifts on special occasions such as: Valentine's Day, Christmas, and New Year. If you do not have the patience (or the time) to stick to Jewelry Making all-year long, why not concentrate just on these occasions for now?

That way, you will only be designing, and creating your designs as you have the time Make one or two pieces a week or month, as time and finances allow and, as the occasion nears, post pictures on your site or your social media pages. People can buy directly that way.

Alternatively, post examples on your site or social media page in order to drum up interest. Giving it at least a month's lead time, ask people to place their orders and pay in advance. A month or so before the occasion, you and your family will be very busy in making the orders. The pre-ordering method for seasonal ventures is very effective because no materials will be wasted. It can also be applied to a year-round venture.

Endless Possibilities with the Target Market

Who wears jewelry? Answer: Everyone.

And no, it's not an exaggeration. You can argue that some people just don't wear jewelry often but, at one point or another, they will be required to wear a piece. Everyone wears jewelry, some more so than others and more often than others.

You can categorize your target market into two sections: Male and Female. Under these main headings, there will be endless sub-categories, especially for women. Let's have a brief analysis of the target market under the women category:

Kids: Who says that it's only adults who want to appear fashionable? Kids nowadays (especially those with young parents) want to have accessories, too! Parents love dressing their kids up so there is even a market for jewelry for small children. Make the jewelry bright and really adorable and you will be on to a winner.

Young students: Those who are still studying also opt for jewelry. Most of the time, the designs are on the simple side, with pleasant colors and not so expensive materials. The advantage is that, though they might not have as much money to spend, they do tend to also have less that they need to spend what money they do have on. They are likely to be willing and able to buy jewelry, especially when it looks unique and cool.

Single ladies: Depending on their lifestyle (do they often stay at home, or they party all night?), their taste in designs will also vary. You should also keep in mind that accessories for work are very important. In a formal office environment, men will wear ties but the ladies will look for elegant, under-stated jewelry. They will also want more casual pieces to wear at the weekend and more fun pieces to wear when they go out on the town.

In a relationship: What can be more appealing to them than couple accessories? That means you have to create the pieces in pairs, one for her, and one for him. Couples, especially new couples, are great news for the jewelry industry - jewelry is a time-honored gift.

Aside from these, we still have women who are married, who are already mothers, those career ladies working as executives who often attend black-tie events. And don't forget those who are grandmothers. Engaging in Jewelry Making Business will truly keep you busy!

Wide Product Niches

As for the products, have no fear because you will never run out of options. Just look at yourself in a full-body mirror. You can have jewelry from your head, down to your toes.

Here are the most popular jewelry types that customers are looking for:

Necklaces: Necklaces can be categorized according to their length, and the level of decoration on them. There are chokers (a necklace that sits high in the neck), matinee necklaces (a necklace that sits on top of the cleavage), and princess necklaces (slightly shorter than the matinee necklace). Necklaces can also plunge beyond the cleavage towards the belly. You can have understated necklaces, delicate necklaces, statement necklaces - the choices are endless.

Arm Jewelry: Who said that you can only adore your arm with bracelets? Don't discount on the other types like cuff links and bangles. Even your upper arm can be adorned with an armlet!

Rings: Rings are very versatile. There can be friendship rings, engagement rings, wedding bands, class rings, promise rings and championship rings.

Brooches: Even your clothes can be adorned with jewelry in the form of brooches.

Legs: Don't forget the anklets and the toe rings.

Other types of jewelry: And just when you thought that jewelry types end there, there still are amulets, charms, prayer beads, lockets, and hair ornaments.

What product niche do you think will suit you best for your business?

Chapter 8: Scaling your Jewelry Making Business

Scaling Defined

In business, when scaling is mentioned, it typically means a good thing. It means that the profits are increasing, but the costs of production (or the capital) are not changing, or, if they are changing , these changes are insignificant or on a downward trend. For example: Your jewelry making business earned $1000 same month last year, and the original investment was only $350. This year, same month, your earnings reached $1500, and you only used $400.

It sounds promising, right? Most business owners aim to scale their business from time to time, but the question is, in Jewelry Making, how will you do that?

4 Surefire Tips To Scale Your Jewelry Making Business

Scaling up your Jewelry Making Business sounds harmless, but the truth is, if you do not do it right, you may risk your business' reputation. Think of the customers and how will they react, if for no apparent reason, you started increasing the prices of your pieces. They will surely feel confused at best, and angry at worst. If they become angry, they may refrain from buying at your shop.

You cannot afford to lose customers just because you want to unreasonably scale up your business. How can you be sure that your scaling is headed on the right direction? Follow these 5 simple tips:

Collect as much positive feedback as possible: Gathering positive feedback is the best form of building your brand. Usually, customers will provide you with it readily, but there are times when you need have to ask them for it. The positive feedback should mostly be about the pieces (that's why it is very important for you to come up with high quality works), but other aspects can also be rated, like the customer service, reliable delivery, and beautiful packaging. As the positive feedback mounts up, post it on your site.

Why is it important in scaling? Simple. By the time you scale up the prices, the customers will already value you and more readily agree with your decision. They will believe that you earned that right because you provide them with quality jewelry and excellent service. This way, they will continue to buy your pieces despite the hike in price.

Your designs should improve and become more varied: As your experience grows, your designs will also be more beautiful and more complicated. The price, of course, also needs to increase. And because the capital in designing is your time, you won't need to add more money in the operating costs.

When customers see that your designs are improving, they will more willingly accept your increase in price. Ask yourself: Will you buy a $65 piece when you know that it is THE SAME $50 jewelry from a year ago? But when you are presented with two pieces made from the same material, one has a simple design, and the other one with more elegant features, you will surely understand the difference in price.

Waste not on materials: When there are left overs in your materials, don't throw them out. After all, they will not expire. If they become old-fashioned, just use them sparingly in your new designs or, where possible, dismantle them to create whole new pieces. Little by little, you will notice that they are becoming out of stock.

Expand: Scaling by increasing the price is good, but doing it while you are finding more customers is even better! New clients won't know what your prices were previously and this can be of great value to you. During the course of your business, don't forget to promote. If you know networks that can garner more clients, join them!

As you expand, you will need more workers, more materials, more time, and more money. This is the time that scaling is extremely necessary. The only rule: do not compromise on quality.

Chapter 9: Increasing Your Profits Without Changing Your Prices

If you feel that you clients are already too price sensitive, you need to look for other ways to make more money. The best way to do this is to look for ways to improve efficiency and cut costs. In this chapter, we will look at both.

Consider Hiring An Assistant

I know what you are thinking - aren't we supposed to be cutting costs? We want to cut costs were it makes sense to but we can increase costs if it means increasing production.

Look at it this way - let us say that you can make 10 necklaces a day at most. That is great. You can sell up to 300 necklaces in a month. Even if you sell all the necklaces, there is no way that you are able to make anymore. The solution then, if you want your business to grow, is to get help.

If you are a bit worried about the cost, why not look into hiring a virtual assistant? You can post a job on one of the freelancer sites like Upwork.com or Guru.com and hire a virtual assistant for the fraction of the cost of a personal assistant. This is perfectly possible and an work well thanks to cloud technology and Skype. They could take care of the administrative functions, allowing you more time to create.

Alternatively, hire someone for specific projects - maybe you can hire someone who will just write the sales blurb and upload your photos.

You could also hire someone to assist you in making up the jewelry. As your business grows, this is going to be something that you have to consider. Let us say that you have someone who is taking care of all the admin for you and you can now make 20 necklaces a day. That is 600 a month - good but still limiting. Take on someone else and teach them to also make 20 necklaces a day and you have doubled your production line.

Buying In Bulk

Buying in bulk can save you quite a bit of money but don't think that it applies only to big wholesalers. Let us say, for example, that you buy hand-crafted glass beads from a one-man shop. Speak to them and see if they would be willing to offer a discount for bulk orders.

Bulk orders can work really well in your favor or they could end up being expensive mistakes so they need the be handled carefully.

You will usually have to buy large amounts of the same thing and so this could mean you ending up with duplicates that you don't use.

Start by looking at generic items that you use, like your findings. You are bound to go through lots of earring hooks, spacer beads, etc. See if you can find these at a wholesale price and you will save a fair amount.

The key to getting bulk buying right is to do it with care - money spent on bulk items cannot be spent on anything else. If it can be used somewhere else more efficiently, it is not time to bulk buy.

Saving Time

I am not going to talk about cutting costs as such because there is a very good chance that you have already been running your business as efficiently as you can when it comes to expenses. Most of us do.

What I am going to talk about here is saving time. This is something that we often forget about - time is money and when you are wasting time, you are literally wasting money as well.

Have a look at your daily work schedule - do you optimize tasks like handling shipping and going to the bank? Are you running to ship items two or three times a day? Make sure that your daily and weekly routines make sense in terms of time wastage.

Next, look at the actual products that you make and work out, product by product, how much each costs in terms of time taken. It may pay you to cut back on some lines or increase the prices accordingly. Let us say, for example, that you make a necklace that is quite intricate in terms of work - perhaps not many materials are used but the necklace takes an hour to make and you make a profit on it of $10. A different necklace may take 20 minutes and only earn $5 profit. Which is the most profitable item?

The necklace that takes an hour to make allows you to earn a profit of $10 for that hour. In that same time, you could have made three of the other necklaces, earning a profit of $15 for that hour. Still think that time doesn't matter?

Chapter 10: Understanding Your Jewelry Making Style and Strengths

To be successful in any business, you need to acknowledge your strengths and weaknesses. Take me, for example, I am a very bad cook - I can bake a mean apple pie but don't ask me to even cook oatmeal, Ill burn it. For me then to open a catering business would be a really bad idea.

Have a look at what you are good at when it comes to jewelry making and build on that. I am not saying that you should never try new things but, when it comes to your business, stick to the things that you are good at and spend the most time on these.

There are many tactics that you can use to play to your strengths and I have listed a few below.

Enjoying Limited Runs

When I say limited runs, I means that you work with just one specific group of gems or stones. You just want to work with beaded charms using only gems that are birthstones, fore example. One of the main advantages of this approach is quickness in building a profile. Because you cater to just one group, people will often approach you if what they are looking for is the product you have. It allows you to set yourself up as an expert in the field - people can see that you concentrate on one speciality and you gain credibility for that. The downside is you have more chance of being negatively effected when it comes to market shortages of supplies, and of course, lack of variety.

Most starting jewelry maker practised this style in one way or another as a way of testing the waters.

Offering One of a Kind Crafts

In this style, you just make one piece of each design and never replicate it- giving your customer a sense that it's the only piece in the whole world. It may sound simple, but it is very challenging. Your piece has to be TRULY unique, not just in your portfolio, but also when compared to other jewellers' creations.

This is the style perfect for those who usually have the knack in designing one of a kind artisan pieces. That is, when they design, other designers will really have a difficulty in replicating it.

The up side is that it has a greater potential to get a higher price. The downside is finding the customer for it and that you have to create different designs for every piece that you make. Most of the time, jewellers who embrace this style go to exhibitions and galleries just to showcase their works.

Should you bundle?

Bundling is the opposite of *One of a Kind Artisan Pieces*. In this style, you'll have many pieces bearing the same design. This style is also profitable, especially if the design you have is sought after by certain customers.

Most jewellers also opt for this type because customers are easy to find. For example, a wedding party want to send a token to their female sponsors-- if they see your pieces and think that it's good, they will order in bundles.

As for individual customers, make it more appealing by indicating exactly how many pieces you have created.

NOTE: Make sure that your designs are still unique compared to other shops. If they see something that is similar to your design and they believe that their price is better than yours, they won't patronize your products.

Embracing Customization - Work with your customers!

A style that is quickly gaining popularity, customization is very promising. In this style, you work with your customers. Either you will take an existing design and they will modify it, or they will ask you to design something completely new for them.

The up side is, the more pieces you customize, the more chances of building your profile: customers will know you as the shop that turn their designs into reality. Downside: it takes more time than usual, so be sure to price accordingly.

Chapter 11: Understanding What People Want to Buy

The heart and soul of your jewelry business are the customers. They will be the ones to appreciate and critique you. The power of their recommendation (or lack thereof) can make or break your business.

Over the years, peoples priorities have changed and so have their expectations. For example, most customers prefer not to spend a lot of time in shops so they opt to look at online catalogues first before going to the store. And when they become extremely busy (or lazy), they may even prefer to order online. No hassle at all. In this example, the customers are buying convenience. Other customers want to see and touch something that they are buying, especially if it is something like expensive jewelry.

Understanding what your customers want is the difference between success and failure.

What Inspires Customers?

First and foremost, what makes your customer want to buy something, particularly the jewelry that yo are selling? This is a very, very vague subject because an inspiration can be anything from the latest blockbuster movie to a wedding proposal.

Their inspiration should also be your inspiration in designing and creating. You can narrow down those inspirations. Perhaps you can just make wedding rings, or focus on casual fashion accessories. When your business is big enough, you need to broaden your scope.

In your website or social media account, make sure that you separate those inspirations into pages, folders, or may be, add a search filter. People will usually filter things to match their own criteria so make your filters match what they might look for. These inspirations can be:

Price - Group jewelry according to its price

According to the jewelry type - Bracelets, necklaces, rings etc.

According to their adornment/stones - Silver, diamond, gemstones, etc.

Purpose - as a gift, for fashion, an investment, etc.

According to collections - Birthstones collection, Blue Collection, Metro, Classic, etc.

When they come in set - Matching necklaces, earrings, bracelets, and rings

The bottom line is, customer inspirations are endless and it has to reflect in your folders, pages or filters. For an instance, a piece of necklace can be categorized as the following:

under the $100 price

something with silver adornment

suited as a gift for her

under a certain collection

it also comes with matching accessories

You have to sort your piece of jewelry to as many categories as possible so that they would not miss it out when searching.

Types of Jewelry Customers

Task-Oriented Customers: These people do not have the time to lurk in the shop, to get their attention you are require to make it more convenient for them by having a website or page where they can select and order. For them, as long as they get the task done, then it's okay.

Value-Seekers: They will have all the time in the world to ask questions about your pieces, so you have to be prepared with answers. To attend to them, make sure your portfolio pictures have accompanying detailed description of the piece. Be very attentive with them because they often shop for more once they see that you have great quality pieces along with excellent customer service. If you can get them on your side, they will be great advocates for your business.

Price-Oriented: They look for pieces that have the lowest price. Be careful with them because most of the time, they are one-time customers only, hence their refusal to spend more than necessary. I am not saying give them bad service but a price-oriented client can be one of the most painful - they will expect the world and a discount at the same time. If anything goes wrong, they will be the first to shout refund and leave bad feedback.

Please note that these are not the only form of customers you will encounter. The rule when handling any type of customer is this: as much as possible, help them find what they are looking for (if it's not in your shop, offer an alternative), and don't lie by exaggerating the value of the pieces.

Chapter 12: Structuring your Jewelry Pricing (and bundling)

How do most jewellers calculate what their jewelry will retail at? They double the production cost! Is it wrong? Not really, because at the end of the day, you've made profits. It is a standard practice that craftspeople use because it can be tough to determine what value of your actual creativity is. They often do themselves a disservice in this manner.

Here is a step by step guide on how to price your jewelry:

Step 1 - Cost of Product

Your product cost is the cost of your basic supplies and any incidental costs that were incurred in making them. If you had to go a few towns over to fetch a special length of chain, the gas used and the time taken are part of this calculation.

Step 2 - Labor cost

Have a dry run, see how much time it will take you to finish one piece. Be sure that when timing, all the materials needed are already within your reach. How much is your time worth? Figure out what you would realistically like to earn per hour in order to live comfortably - minus the yacht and private jet please.

Step 3 - Start computing!

The formula is actually simple:

Add the product cost and what it would cost to ship.

Multiply the sum by 2.5 (this part is completely up to you)

Add the labor cost for making one such product

Add another 10% over and above that to get your base price

Here is a quick example.

You had a jewelry made using $5 materials in just 30 minutes

The packaging you used cost a total of $1

Add them together and you will have $6, now multiply it by 2.5

What you'll have is $15

Granted that your hourly rate is $15/hour and it took you just half an hour to finish the piece, then you have to add $7.5 to your $15

You will have $22.5

10% of that is $2.25

Add $22.5 and $2.25: you will have $24.75

$24.75 is your base price, you can sell your pieces using that price. It may seem like a far jump from your $6 start up cost, but if you will sell your jewelry at just $12, you won't be able to STAY in the business for long. Should the time come that you want to scale, customers will feel "cheated" because they already got accustomed to your low price. Compare the price to similar goods on the market and see whether or not it is above or below average. If it is very high compared to other similar goods, you will either need to convince the client of the value of buying your product or will need to reduce the price.

Step 4 - For Wholesale or Bundles

When computing for the wholesale price, you can multiply the sum of materials and packaging to 1.5 instead of 2.5. That way, the price will be reduced from $24.75 to only $18.15.

Chapter 13: How to Market Effectively (Limited Time Bonus Chapter)

Marketing or promoting your pieces is crucial. Say, you have very good jewelry with an outstanding design, but you lack the skill in promoting the product, your efforts will be wasted. There should be an equal effort in creating your products and in marketing them.

Listed below are the most effective marketing techniques to make your jewelry pieces popular:

Social Media Marketing: The best way to make people notice your work is to send it their way. Social networking sites are powerful: you just have to be patient in creating a portfolio and strategically sharing information about your products.

Social media marketing is a fine balance - overdo it and people will think that you are just spamming them. The way to win at social media marketing is to get people to look forward to what you are sharing.

Create a business page for your business - this is free and post to it no more than once or twice a day at most. Use the 80/ 20 principle here. Share information with your prospective market that has no sales message at all 80% of the time. You should only market to them 20% of the time.

This is good advice so heed it. Doing things this way gives clients the impression that you actually care about them and are not just interested in selling them something. If you are constantly trying to sell something to them, they will ignore your message and block your page. NOT good.

If you provide useful information about things that they are interested in, they will look forward to reading your posts and even share them. This is an effective way to get people talking about your page.

With Facebook ads, you set your own budget - even as little as a dollar a day will work. Facebook allows you to target your adds in terms of sex, location, age, interests, etc. so you can really put your ads in front of the right target market. They also provide tools to allow you to analyze how effective your ads were and this is really great to learn from.

PPC Ads: These are a little more expensive than Facebook ads but are displayed across a much wider forum. You offer to pay a certain amount per click and then set an overall budget. When someone clicks on your ad, you have to pay. It is better to offer a reasonable amount per click - at least $0.75 because Google will give preference to higher click values and your ad will appear higher in search engine results.

Widen your horizon: Join organizations, websites, blogs and forums that have a to jewelry. Most of them will allow you to promote. For an instance, a blog about fashion will welcome jewelry posts, and a website about entrepreneurship would accept posts with portfolio pictures as long as the contents are related to entrepreneurship. Be active, and watch your number of followers increase.

While posting in those blogs, websites, or forums, don't forget to link the audience back to your website.

Give back to customers: You can also promote by holding a contest. Ask existing customers to "model" your crafts. The process goes like this: they will take a picture of when they are wearing your jewelry, they will send it to you, and you will post it on your website/social media account. Whoever garners the most likes will win a very unique gift, or if you can afford it, a monetary prize.

Your customers will work hard to find as many likes as possible, and in doing so, they will be promoting your other pieces.

Sponsor Events: If there is a fashion event, grab that opportunity to promote your pieces. All you need to do is let the models borrow your jewelry so they will walk down the catwalk wearing it. The models and those who will see them wearing it are bound to ask if the jewelry pieces they see are really great.

Welcome resellers: If you want others to market your work, then open up for reselling. You can do this by letting the reseller buy your pieces in bulk, give them a discount, and they will sell the jewelry at a price the same as yours. For them to sell, they will of course promote your crafts.

Just be clear on your grounds in reselling, and terminate a reseller if he or she violates your rules. For example, they cannot sell your pieces at a higher price than you have recommended, and they should only sell using your business name. That means they will be required to use your packaging boxes and bags.

Wear it proud: Last but not the least, be sure to promote your crafts by wearing them. Each person you meet is a potential customer, so don't be complacent by wearing other brands!

In the end you should not forget the basic tips like making sure your photos are of high quality and that when customers ask, complain, or demand, you will be there to listen and take action. Word of Mouth is also very powerful. If you offer them great pieces along with great service, people will promote your brand, free of charge.

Chapter 14: Selling Your Jewelry Online and doing it Profitably

Physical stores are great if you already have the capability and the finances to open one up, but if you are still not prepared for that venture, you have to make the most out of selling online.

How can you sell your pieces online, safely and profitably? Follow the simple tips below:

Accurate shipping information: Check the shipping information twice or thrice before sending the package. You cannot afford to lose both money and customer just because the package did not arrive on time, or because it arrived at the wrong doorstep!

The right craft to the right customer: It may be an elementary mistake, but it happens so do not take it lightly. Check if the jewelry you are sending is indeed the jewelry that the customer has ordered!

Consider this- If a customer sent you a message that says you delivered the wrong item, you have two choices: a) you will ask the customer to send the item back, which will definitely inconvenience them, or b) you will give the item for free and send her original order. Whatever you choose, you are bound to lose profits because of the shipping costs!

Reliable packaging: Some customers are picky. They do not want their items to be jostled too much, so you must make sure that they are securely packaged. This also prevents them from receiving damaged jewelry, so invest in good packaging with your business name and contact details on it. If it's possible, send a brochure in every delivery you make.

Remember the Proof!

Did you ever experience this frustrating scenario: you have paid for the item in a timely manner but it was delivered to you in a late fashion? When you confronted the seller, she told you that she "thought" you had still not paid.

Don't do that to your buyers. To help you become organized, once payment is made, list the order down under the "to be shipped" folder. Don't let it sit in your laptop or PC for long. You risk forgetting about it! Once the order has been shipped, highlight it with color yellow (or any color that you want). Don't forget to inform the buyer that the order has already been forwarded to the shipping agency.

Through all these, make sure that you keep the proof: from earliest possible conversation, to payment and to proof of shipping. They will come in handy in case the customer complains about something.

Broaden your payment options

Not all customers have credit cards, so do not make that your only payment method. Look around you: are there remittance centers? Don't forget to accept payment through bank deposits. When you are established enough, may be you can start initiating cash-on-delivery methods.

Flexibility in payment options will make the customers more inspired to buy because they can choose the payment method that is most convenient for them.

Be flexible in shipping - But have a cut off schedule!

To save money in shipping, be sure to have a schedule. For example: You always ship items daily, but for the customer's item to be shipped right away, payment proof should be sent not later than 12 pm. If the payment is made later than that, then you will only be able to ship her item the next day.

This routine will help you stay organized. When all the payments for the day are in, you can start arranging the packages, checking the shipping addresses, and making sure that they are securely snug in their boxes. By around 2 pm, you will be able to peacefully go to the shipping station, certain that you have not forgotten anything.

Chapter 15: The Best "Alternative" Jewelry Making Resources

The following can serve as additional references for your jewelry making business:

Books

How to Start a Home-Based Jewelry Making Business, By Maire Loughran

This book will teach you how to make a living out of your passion in making jewelry. Not much tips on how to create jewelry, but great tips in making jewelry business plans.

The Handmade Marketplace: How To Sell Your Crafts Locally, Globally, And Online, by Kari Chapin

Also about different strategies on how to sell, but this time, it emphasizes on different avenues of selling online (Etsy, e-Bay, etc). There are also tips on how to start your own website, and how to arrange your pieces for a portfolio-perfect picture!

Forums

Jewelry Making Daily: A complete forum you can join where you can find topics like where to buy supplies, step by step jewelry making instructions, competitions, events and classes.

http://www.jewelrymakingdaily.com/forums/

Bella Online: It is actually a general website for women, but they offer a separate forum for jeweller making. There are many useful topics like metal smithing, how-to's in jewelry making, and planning for an exhibit.

http://forums.bellaonline.com/ubbthreads.php?ubb=postlist&Board=203

Websites

Jewelry Making Journal: This site contains useful information from creating jewelry (free tutorials), pricing them, and then making sales.

http://jewelrymakingjournal.com/start-a-jewelry-business/

All Free Jewelry Making: This website has free e-Books to offer, and it even comes with a blog containing many useful articles. For those looking for bead buys, this one also has an online bead shop.

http://www.allfreejewelrymaking.com/

Conclusion

Thank you again for downloading this book!

I do hope that this book has been useful as a guide to starting your own jewelry business. Perhaps you are feeling a little overwhelmed at all the information but that is completely normal - reread whatever chapters you fell that you need to recap.

All that is left now is for you to get started. Remember, you are a successful seller once you have sold your first item - selling your first item means that you got it right and it should inspire you to carry on.

Even if you can only, at this stage, make this a part-time business, I urge you to get started. There is life outside of the grey little office cubicles - it's time for you to get free of them.

One last thing, if you don't mind - Would you take a few minutes to review this book on Amazon for me? I would greatly appreciated hearing your thoughts.

Thank you and the very best of luck!

Made in the USA
San Bernardino, CA
28 November 2018